Inside Out

a collection of poetry + prose
by meg junky

meg junky

Copyright © 2020 Megan C. Junkermeier

All rights reserved. This book or any portion thereof may not be reproduced or used in any manner whatsoever without the written permission of the author except for the use of brief quotations in articles or reviews.

ISBN: 9798634551470

inside out

i write so i can breathe
these thoughts need air
and so do i

meg junky

the scent of fresh ink on a new page

- soul work

inside out

i sprinkle words into these poems
like rose petals onto the bed
you gather as many as your hands can hold

meg junky

daydreaming of you
is like a perfect day in may
bees cheer
birds rejoice
flowers celebrate
gleaming at the beauty surrounding us
contentment after a grueling winter
peace after a troubling journey
fully present and not concerned
with anything at all
how wonderful it is
to be alive and thinking of you

inside out

my daddy tells this story
of when i was just a little girl
it was summertime at my first home
in the evening
the moon was bigger and brighter
than i had ever seen before
its brilliance glowing above
fearlessly
magnificently
so i ran down the driveway
naturally
honestly
i reached my arms out to hold it
and he said he smiled
the way he does each time he tells the story
because that's when he knew
my dreams would travel to other galaxies
my ambitions would reach for the stars
one glance
and i recognized the moon

meg junky

last night i told the moon about you
and she glowed a little brighter

inside out

my favorite time
to be alive in minnesota
is at 8:00 in the evening in june
i sit on the porch step
the sun is preparing its trip
among a pink and orange sky
the trees wave - gifting to me a breeze
the cardinals call - offering me a seat
the robins chatter - telling me of their days
it all seems so effortless to them
pleased just to be here
perched on the branches
beneath cotton candy clouds
no complaints
no worries
only song
so innocent
so sweet
and sometimes - at 8:03 in the evening in june
i wonder if you and i could be birds

i thought i saw
the first letter
of the first word
from the sentence you were about to say
twirling on the tip of your tongue
before reeling backward on the stage
behind the curtain of your lips
and hiding in your cheek
but for a second
i saw it
and i feel it too

inside out

i melt like a sundae in july
at the thought
of your hand grazing mine
the tips of your fingers
telling the tips of mine truths
you are not ready to use your lips for
but still want to say

meg junky

chemistry
a language
two understand
no more
no less
confident
uninhibited
passion
cannot be taught
it is there
or it is not
wait my darling
you'll see

inside out

the space between your gaze and mine says it all

- connection

meg junky

i get lost in your smile
the one you make right before you laugh
do you even know that is your soul saying hello

inside out

when you dream
and no one can see but you
am i anywhere to be found
or is it me who is dreaming of you

for awhile it felt like my voice evaporated with the morning dew. and i, a mere blade of grass, kept steady and still. i was trampled. i was cut. i rose again. winter after winter i prevailed the cold. i fought through fallen autumn leaves from underneath the trees. looking back, i cannot quite tell what made it go. no one event to point to in particular. and as i sit in the stillness now, i am pondering and coming up short. however, what i can say now is this: many clues have trickled down over time like the rain upon the grass. the most important said: create for you. create because it is what you must do to feel alive. create because you feel it rising from your bones. create because you cannot breathe unless you do. create. for. you. remember: art lives in your soul. it is an expression of your truth. and who are any of us to judge another's truth? remember this feeling when the winter comes and your soul is cold. remember to never stop creating. remember to not worry about opinions or criticisms of your art, of your truth. your soul deserves a place to share its creations. remember: it is not they who felt their voice lost. it is not they who discovered it again.

inside out

one look and i am starstruck by your face
one touch and i am sent into outer space

- astronaut

we scribbled love notes back and forth
in a hotel room
i gathered them like seeds and took them
home to bloom

inside out

inspiration lies inside the space
where my atoms see your atoms
and want everything to do with them

meg junky

why were we given an ability to *desire* so much
when we are cursed with a reality
where it goes unfulfilled

inside out

you said you thought you would keep me around
for a while. too bad i got in the way.

meg junky

oh, the burn of my saturn return
still yet to discern what i have to learn

inside out

i am a choreographer of words
paper
my stage
pen
my dancer
heart
my music

- sit back and enjoy the show

meg junky

your dream
a dandelion seed
floating in the wind
seemingly small
but infinitely capable
of soaring into the breeze
and building something
far greater than itself

inside out

there is nothing
WILDER
than your *imagination*

(except mine)

meg junky

sometimes i wonder
if you have ever
really
really
really
been in love
i have tasted
its pure nectar
its sweet sunshine
its spellbinding tonic
and i can't go back now

inside out

when does
in love
become
love
and which do we prefer

meg junky

this afternoon
i rinsed the sea's salt
from sun-bathed curls
and washed the white sand
from between my toes
i returned them to the ocean
where they belong
only the freckles on my cheeks
and the sweet memories will remain
everything will go back to where it came from
just like you

- summer romance

inside out

what a simple life the flowers have
they draw in the sun's rays
thanking them in a myriad of colors
they greet the bees and butterflies
embracing them in a kind hug
they drink the cool rain water
quenching their patient thirst
they sleep under the stars each night
dreaming of a never-ending summer
oh, how i wish to live among the peonies

meg junky

i cannot believe my eyes
a wonderland like this
is this real
am i dreaming
this is absolute bliss
can we stay near the mountains for a while
watch the grass grow and the snow fall
this unbelievable view
the crisp clean air
i want it all
the earth is a never-ending wonder
she reminds me to be grateful for everything
above my head and under
for the ground i walk upon
for the air i breathe
for the food i eat and the water i drink
without her i could not live at all
without her my heart could not beat
i want to live inside the beauty
i want to watch her paint the view anew
over and over
as we grow older

inside out

black and white photographs
speak to me honestly
telling me rich stories
with more life in evermore shades
than their cousins of colour
sharing intimate details
uncovering truths
leaving you *lingering* in question
i fall in love with each one

meg junky

my heart expands in paris
my appetite thrives in sicily
my dreams adventure in lima
my honesty spreads in london
my spirit blossoms in bengaluru
my sensuality blooms in barcelona

i left pieces of myself
to grow in these cities
and for this
i am glad

- a traveler's tale to me

inside out

if i can write these kinds of words
just thinking about you
imagine what i could write
actually having you

- imagination

meg junky

i think you could drive me crazy
in all the ways i want to be driven crazy

inside out

i find myself bewitched
by the night sky
stars fixed
possibilities fly
comforted
in knowing why
a future hid
will satisfy
unfulfilled
til drawing nigh
it shows itself

meg junky

i write words to you
sentences glued with longing
hoping that someday i will be
brave enough to share them
but today
is not that day
so instead i put ~~lines~~ through them
and tear them up
until they are letters scattered across the table
sentences no more
words disappeared
and all their meaning
sent back to me

inside out

some songs dig deep into your lungs
and pull your breath out from under you

meg junky

i think about you so often the wind whispers your
name in my ear as i walk along the sidewalks

inside out

catching memories
like fireflies
an open jar on my knee
i see them glowing above
traveling in all directions
one chance i have for each one
i know this like most things in life
and on this summer night
they fly freely
reminding me
why they do
and why all i have left
are memories

meg junky

she is like the morning dew
and the sun-streaked lilies in the garden

inside out

my tangled hair
holds many secrets
each strand a tale of its own
come closer
sit near the water with me
unveil your ocean eyes
under this rose gold sky
and i'll share a few with you

meg junky

i am waiting for the one
a drop in the ocean
sending ripples through my waters
with tender motion

i am waiting for the one
a breeze on my shoulder
reminding me he is here
with every year older

i am waiting for the one
a leaf on the tree
cascading down from above
falling just to greet me

i am waiting for the one
a ray on my cheek
kissing me with warmth
when the day is bleak

i am waiting for the one
a loving soul mate
unique to me
entrusted to fate

inside out

he was comfortable in his chaos
knowing his world whirled faster than any other
and even if he could not keep up
he could not get hurt
before he really truly wanted something
it would already be gone
you can't miss something you never had
sweet evasion
he flew through his days
like wind through the mountains
dazed and twirling through life
and time moved on
one day
years later
he looked down at his hands
skin worn and wrinkled
sun spots and all
tears streamed down his face
as he wondered
what have i done
he missed everything he never had
he missed her
sweet evasion

meg junky

there is a tidal wave
flowing inside my brain
step into the water baby
don't let it be in vain

with every breath i take
the ocean sweeps me away
further into this sea dream
can we just stay here and play

inside out

as i visited my childhood home
the second one to be exact
i could sense the presence of you
even though you're somewhere else
i looked at the oak trees
they used to be green
now aging and brittle
like memories of you
we used to play beneath them
and run around in the yard
i used to teeter totter with you
and you would swing with me
how did we get here?
how did you end up there?
i used to hug you whenever i wanted
and sit next to you there
it is a strange thing to be in your room
and in this house at all
i haven't been here since you left
it was too hard to be here
after six years i have returned
and so have the tears

meg junky

how can you be gone?
i never thought you'd leave
do you know how much i miss you?
i wonder if you miss me
you had too few years here
i wish i could have known
all the songs we used to sing
and all the songs we could have
you still live within these walls
even though you live behind others now
i see all these versions of you here
in all the framed photographs
they may see you differently now
but i still see you clearly
our stories live in the trees
like pages inside of books
the playhouse remembers you
it whispered to me your name
i remember all of it (i hope you do too)
i remember you (i hope you do too)

inside out

there is grace in water
it cleanses you
no matter how dirty
it hydrates you
no matter how thirsty
it refreshes you
no matter how tired
it cools you
no matter how warm
however you came
it will be there for you
for you are of it and it is of you

- elements, part one

meg junky

the weather is perfect today
70s
sunshine
and a light breeze
now all i need is you

- may day

inside out

skin
a stained glass window
dancing
an array of colors

heart
a newly awoken sunflower
tilting
brilliant and yellow

sun
a warm familiar face
blessing
the other two

meg junky

try as i might
i have no power to stop
the thoughts of you entering my mind
trust me when i say i have been giving it time
though i dream in the day
and i dream in the night
my wishes will not compromise
your lips are on my mind
my lips are yours to find
and each time i see your face
within this darkened place
i try not to look away
i try not to blink if i may
so i don't miss these moments
because i know what will come of this
my memory soon will flake
now it feels like a mistake
to have wished you away
as i held you in my hands
and hoped you would stay

inside out

look closer
your heart is a muscle
unlike all others
small in stature
powerful in delivery

look closer
your mind has more neurons
than stars in the night sky
intricate and vast
spectacular in performance

look closer
your body is a collage
of incredible systems
intertwined and fluid
stunning in movement

meg junky

look closer
your spirit is yearning
for expansion
pure and true
genuine in root

look closer
feel the magnificence
taste the wonder
of the delicate
exceptional
existence
that is you

inside out

it is in our nature to connect
it is in our mind to seek
it is in our heart to grow
it is in our soul to love

meg junky

your art is your soul
slowly undressing
layer by layer
beside your cheerful heart
yearning for truth
pleading to reach out
from underneath the weight
desperate for life
seeking the hand of another
praying to find
an eager soul
aside a blossoming heart
slowly undressing
across the way
ready to share her art too

inside out

i humor myself
and reach for the glass
but we know it will be the bottle
eventually
i never knew how to not drink it all
just like i never knew how to not love all of you

meg junky

you make me feel like i can move mountains
feel like waves of the ocean tide
powerful yet graceful too
in a beautiful swift stride

i am here for you dear
looking inward you'll see
everything you need
already with you, with me

inside out

i know the way your mind works
it is how mine works too

i know the way your heart pulls
it is how mine pulls too

i know the newness you crave
it is what i crave too

i know the curiosity you carry
it is what i carry too

i don't mind that you are not sure
i am not sure too

i know you are a falling star
i know i am falling for you

meg junky

your listening
your comforting
your understanding
you're everything

- mother

inside out

can i weep
with you
for you
while you weep too

- empathy

meg junky

heavy are the chains
invisible to you
but designed by they
who hold the reins

inside out

i crave the space where i know i am alone
the emptiness where my mind is freed
the vastness where my soul can create
this is where i imagine my words
funneling and cascading into poems
this is where i picture my art
formulating and caressing the canvas
this is where the passion thrives
i need the space
to think
to write
to paint
i need the space to create
an artist needs more rooms than you
if you need one then she needs a few
give her the rooms and she will give back to you
she just needs the space
she needs to create

meg junky

if you could see through these eyes
you'll find an unexplainable surprise
although i would advise
to weed through all the lies

let go of your assumptions
give into your temptations
and travel to this nation
with colorful imagination

at once you will unlock doors
questions unanswered before
magical and wondrous love
happiness and joy above

hereafter you will change
this world will seem strange
yet the right ones can relate
to an energy shift so great

inside out

the breeze plays with my hair
a gentle touch on my shoulder
vata energy
i can breathe deeply with you
a most basic ritual
we forget to give thanks
so thank you
for the gift of today
you give me life
i am attached to you forever
without you i am nothing

- elements, part two

meg junky

before i side with any of you
i must hear their tales
it is my duty
it is my right
it has been this way since birth
to stand together
to empower one another
i must hear their stories
i must answer their call
it is the only way we will make it through

- sisterhood

inside out

she is bruised and tired
she is burned and snapped
she is twisted and trampled
she is pummeled and whacked
she is plowed and stained
she is raked and looted
she is traded and borrowed
she is torn and polluted

if she was your sister
your wife or your grandmother
you could not stand
to read these lines one after another

but this is a tale of our matriarch true
and the fight for her life must continue

- mother earth

meg junky

the pendulum has swung one way far too long
force built on this side far too great to stand by
here - it - comes
hurricanes
wildfires
melted glaciers
yet we continue
breeding livestock for slaughter
feeding seven billions hunger
decapitating trees for lumber
stealing breath out from under
living on borrowed time we plunder
we need bees to pollinate
the ones we decimate
the forest seethes
we need trees to breathe
the clock is ticking

inside out

slay the trees
rape the earth
suffocate the oceans

buy your yachts
fly your private jets
trade your billions of dollars

your money
will
not
save
you
when we are all dead

meg junky

the opposite of love
is not hate
it is fear

- oppression

inside out

we fancy ourselves
the superior species
yet we are the ones
who kill out of malice
who feast for pleasure
who destroy because we can
now tell me
how
is that
superior?

meg junky

money is still the root of all evil

inside out

your words make me burn like blazing fire
when all i ever intended to be was water

- chemical reactions

Call for Change

we have waited while you have lied
we have stood with our hands tied
we have cried out for fair wages
we have searched news pages
we have heard promises tattered
we have seen oceans battered
we have endured the pain
we have mourned the slain
we are calling out once and for all
we are standing up we are standing tall

do not fail us in our triumphant cry
do not think we will stand by
do not forget you were once young too
do not pretend there is nothing to do
do not ignore the climate strikes
do not crumble under our dislikes
do not hide behind your tenured time
do not accept a corrupted dime
do not assume we will stand down
do not get comfortable with your crown

inside out

we will rise above your tainted soil
we will rise above your sick turmoil
we will rise above your fried billboards
we will rise above your oily swords
we will rise above your fossil fuel towers
we will rise above your futile powers
we will rise above your processed speeches
we will rise above your lobbying leeches
we will rise above your financial schemes
we will rise to reach our dreams

meg junky

you will be waiting a lifetime
for the apology
he never learned to give

inside out

everyone i meet
has a child within
sitting
waiting patiently
on the front step of their hearts
just waiting to be asked:
do you want to play?

- inner child | likeness

meg junky

your nervous system will tell you what love isn't
long before your heart catches up

inside out

lately i crave the silence
the
s p a c e
between
my thoughts
my heart
my mind

and you

meg junky

these days
i find myself
sifting through silences
like a panhandler for gold
those words
are not here
spilling from your lips
like they used to
anymore

inside out

'your eyes are so expressive'
how could i forget such a line
you used to look at me
with a gaze so divine
it was your superpower i believe
to look and to really see
but i promise i know
we are where we are meant to be
me - no longer with you
you - no longer with me

meg junky

i dream that you are behind a door
and i do not have the key
i knock and pull
and scream your name
you are nowhere to be found

i dream that you are behind a window
and i cannot slide the glass
i push and pound
and scream your name
you are nowhere to be found

i dream that you are sitting in front of me
and i cannot reach you
i lean and grasp
and scream your name
you are nowhere to be found

i wake up and see no one and nothing
i cannot reach you
i run and call
and scream your name
you are nowhere to be found

inside out

needn't i mention
i am paralyzed with tension
your continual dissention
not paying attention
our evaporating connection
relationship mutation
leaves me in suspension
attempted communication
innocent misinterpretation
undying frustration
souls in hypertension
praying for ascension
what was your intention
because mine was transcension

meg junky

i painted you an angel
as i was filled with mirth
now i see another angle
perspective in rebirth
from delusion i untangle
as you descend down to earth
truth, though always gainful
leaves me questioning your worth

inside out

her skin
soft like rose petals
her honeysuckle lips
decorate her as her tulip hips dip
how can he touch her
with those sandpaper hands
what a sin to scrape her skin
his touch with no intention to love
this exterior man wants too much
and gives too little
he has no interior span
carelessly devouring is his only plan
just watch and see
how rose petals fall from his lips
and honey drips from his chin
he is drunk off her skin
while she hides
within

if he doesn't see you
when everyone else does
he never will

- you should not have to beg for love

inside out

how are we so quick to dissent in our confidence
and agree with the disdain of our very own
character under the wicked spell of those who
have no care for our flourishing futures or
budding potentials?

- your opinion is the one that matters

meg junky

tears ran down my cheeks until i fell asleep
and in the morning with a thunder warning
rain streamed from the sky
i see mother heard my cry

inside out

i am not here for you
not your staples, not your glue

i am not a handbag or a sack
in which to hold your feelings back

i am not on this earth to breathe
the air stuck between your teeth

i am not a guide to show the way
to point on a map the places to stay

i am not your motivator
a person to resent later

i am not your spiritual leader
to turn you into a better reader

i am not your therapist
here to douse you in existential mist

meg junky

i am not what you need
so here i stand and here i plead

to see what it is you do
i am not here for you

inside out

can you see the flames
she angers just like us

can you feel the rain
she cries just like us

can you see the wind
she runs just like us

can you feel the sun
she warms just like us

can you see the ocean
she heals just like us

- unity

meg junky

my morning tea warms me more
than you ever could
and i'm thankful to not be trying so hard anymore

inside out

self-worth
was something i grew up with
and many men have tried to steal

meg junky

this time
when my breath was spent
my courage wilted
and my feet too tired to continue
i looked up to the heavy clouds
until i found it
a thin line of hope
it was there
waiting for me
whenever i could breathe again

- silver lining

inside out

when you crave my fruit
you lather me with compliments
cast your lines in my sea
twirl the reel
and when i don't bite
when i rinse off your words
your ego *roars*
hurdles thundering insults
transforms compliments to criticisms
calling my ripened fruit rotten
simply because
it didn't want your lips

meg junky

some days
i wish i could bury my head
in the sand
like an ostrich
and disappear
with gritty blinded eyes
some nights
i want to turn up the speakers
so loud
and drown
in the sound of emptiness
pillowing disarray
this vacuum of space
this black hole of silence
is deafening

inside out

the trouble is that someday
you will want to own me
to wear me like cufflinks
to wrap me around you
like a winter scarf
to cover yourself with me
like that jacket you love
but save for special occasions
you will offer your price
and calmly i will refuse
in frustration you will fight
for it is me you sought
you try with all your might
but i cannot be bought

meg junky

those who would rather be right
will be alone
those who would rather compromise
will be in love

inside out

subtle alterations
a glance held longer than the last
leads me to sense
that everything i thought i knew
is floating in the wind
and everything that is to come
is rushing in with the rain
the inevitable shift is approaching
you may not see it coming
but i have known of its journey for years
and i must say
i recognize the call
i cannot ignore this sensation
my destiny awaits

meg junky

i wait for the harvest moon
to follow along the groove
of what is to come soon
and what is bound to move

inside out

i am the rich soil you walk upon
i am the ground holding you gently
i am the leaves that fall then crunch
i am the trees gifting the air you breathe
i am the paths leading to the mountains
i am the tulips the daisies and the peonies
i am the calm streams in which you bathe
i am the comfort when you rest under the stars
i am the mother caring for all you see
i am the provider of all you need

- elements, part three

meg junky

it is 7:14 and you are still asleep
i pick up my pen for the daily ritual
you see
these words know when they are ready
they find me
i do not have to call
feelings flow toward the tip
and fill with ink
they are not scared at all
to tell
me
so i tell
you
on these pages
here we are
these letters
and you
and me
naturally from my bones they creep

inside out

you know every move to make
to leave me with no resistance whatsoever

- superpowers

restlessness is familiar to me. we meet on saturday afternoons when neither of us have plans. (he likes to rub it in those days) we sit on the shore where your own life stretches out like the lake into the horizon and you can't help but examine it. we talk over dessert wine, loose and open to admission. we laugh over martinis, sharing old stories. we say hello on mountaintops as we soak in the vastness. and it is here, in the crisp air, i realize that no matter the scenery, or the hour of the day, restlessness and i are more familiar than i like to admit. we know each other's faces. we know the signs. and sometimes, deep into the night, when my head rests softly on my pillow, restlessness comes. we embrace. he stays for a little while - pillow talk. and finally, when it stops, we can hear each other breathing. in. and out. as the clock turns over to the next hour i smile. he winks. he slips into the darkness, and i fall asleep.

inside out

you are not the one this poem is about but you
are here to hear it

- inner conflict

meg junky

you still visit me in my dreams
waiting
knocking
on the corners of my mind
on the door to my heart
is this the only place i will ever see you again?

- loss

inside out

i didn't know it was going to be the last time
when it was
i wish i had a warning
i would have held my breath
and held onto you
wishes are hard to come by these days
and memories are even harder to find
are you happy where you are
i see your face and you look so
but looks can be deceiving
i wonder if you ever think about me
because i think about you
and wishes are hard to come by these days
but i still wonder if maybe
you would grant me one last wish
just this one time

meg junky

my mother always told me
it's that thing called life
and now i am here
standing in the center
and i see just what she means

inside out

lust and love are quarreling teams
a state of confusion i am in it seems
you and i oh how we try
tension builds from here i cry
desire and duty are rarely friends
this tug of war it never ends
black and white now fade away
into shades of grey i stay

meg junky

they don't tell you
how powerful
how wonderful
your body is at first
a hidden secret
until the men come 'round
they want a feel
they desire a taste of your honeysuckle skin
they want a home
they desire a place inside of you
why did no one tell you they were coming
why did no one tell of your womanhood stunning
an explanation of your phenomena
there was no indication
there was no warning
so here i am to say
you are the roses in the garden
vibrant and soft
so here i am warning you
they want to pluck your petals
and if you're not careful
they will tear you off your stems
one by one

inside out

listen
careful whispers
muffled
corner booth
one light
dimmed
two voices
over bitter coffee
hushed
concerned for you
the watchmen
charged with your safety
listen

- inner voice

meg junky

maybe the hard part isn't finding your dream
maybe the hard part is admitting to yourself
how much you want it
and how much you're willing to give up
because some things are only
for you

inside out

break the fairytale in two
where a prince comes to save you
for this is not true
my dear
you are the princess
and the prince
and the horse he rides in on
and the path they ride away on
and the sunset they ride into
and the castle they live in happily ever after
you are every bit of magic there is
and you are as real as real could be

meg junky

do not come crying
i will not wipe tears from your green eyes
when your teeth are rotting from the sugar

do not come crying
i will not wipe tears from your bearded cheeks
when your body is aching from the withdrawal

do not come crying
i will not wipe tears from your tilted brow
when your heart is buried from the emptiness

the roses have gone
there is no love here
you left it behind
and made it disappear

inside out

i see your eyes adjust
to my shade of sunlight
amber mixed with rose petals
you sit next to me at the bar
in a pale blue button-down shirt
loose with two buttons undone
you ask for my name and i hesitate
thinking you must be here
because your life is a little greyed
your skin paler than last season
you've decided you're after a little sun
and my beams struck the corner of your eye
but sir, you see
i have gathered these rays
i have done the work
i have raked this shine
and you have come here to *bask*
to *feed* on this light
you think maybe it's easier to steal my sunshine
than to build yours
but sir, you see, my sunshine ain't free

meg junky

each of us is a puzzle
mismatching pieces
playing the game of life
collecting from those we meet
some needed
some unwanted
and so on and so on and so on
i know of an elusive piece
still missing from mine
i thought it would be from you
yet after all these tries
the twisting and turning
i see it could never fit
not like i thought it would
and it needs to fit
it must
fit

inside out

i misplaced
my pocket guide
for this relationship
these simple phrases
go misunderstood
i thought i could
cover my bases
but now i trip
losing my stride
what a disgrace

meg junky

we know our truth long before
we act on it and begin to live
why must we pretend we don't

- women's intuition

inside out

bad feeling days
make for
good writing days

- process

meg junky

and there
in the kitchen
standing on the cool hardwood
they come
the feelings
the feelings
the feelings
their hunger pulls
they need nourishment
they know
this is where i come to feed
and now
so do they

inside out

here i sit at a stoplight lit
with a flashing yellow
left turn arrow
once again
two options appear
here i sit while both are free
for me and i must choose
but what if i lose
what if i miss
my chance for bliss
what if these moments misalign
from a misinterpreted sign
here i sit and i could stay and pray
or i could turn and burn
my current state is left to fate
here i sit in contemplation
i see both of your faces
and all of the places
we could go and so
here i sit

meg junky

sometimes you must break your life like a twig
SNAP IT
in two
burn the sapling
and announce to the world
i am coming
for you

inside out

my molecules are stirring
my cells are restless
my heart beats for something new
i cannot go around and around again
i cannot be a spoke in a wheel
i am two bare feet
walking softly through sand near the ocean
i am two arms
reaching out at the edge of a mountain's cliff
i am two eyes
looking out and enthralled at beauty herself
i am one soul
set ablaze by the sun itself
i am one mind
learning through unending curiosity
i am one heart
seeking the truth unapologetically
i cannot go around and around again
my heart beats for something new

meg junky

we live in two different worlds
i see beauty all around me
and you can only see what is missing

- foreign language

inside out

tell yourself a secret
one known since birth
you deserve anything
aligning with your worth

remind yourself today
of the journey you are on
your spirit is singing
hear her beautiful song

meg junky

one day you won't have to try
you will breathe in
and the words will rush out
a hurricane
a tsunami
all the things you've waited to say
thoughts waiting for their day
lined up troops marching in formation
toward ears ready to hear
and souls ready to listen
promising emancipation
and your sweet redemption

inside out

i know moments like these
like running your fingers over the flyleaf of an
unbelievable book

- anticipation

meg junky

i see him standing in the kitchen
making coffee
a scent of fresh grounds floating in the air
rays of sun flicker on the pothos leaves
white kitchens are my favorite
they let the *light* in
we can always use more *light*
i see him searching the cupboard
he picks out two mugs
one i got him for his birthday
and one he bought for me
a song leaps off the record player
the music fills the *space*
leaving just enough room
for us

inside out

you are the space
where the sunlight meets the ocean tide
and smiles
tossing her worries aside
and glows
as she makes her stride and his rays take flight

meg junky

some days
i am tired of the city
the noise
the traffic
the chaos
what a pity
give me space
in the nature quiet
and i shall rest
upon a sunshine diet

inside out

my favorite time of day is dusk
when sun and moon share the stage
what a beautiful performance to see

have you ever sat down and made a list of everything you were doing for someone else and everything you were doing for you? which column is the length of the earth's circumference and which column is the length of your pinky nail? why drop yourself off at the doorstep while everyone goes inside? you're out there on the porch while everyone is inside draining you like bottles of red wine at dinner, never noticing the emptiness of your eyes. you only have so much time. one day, you might burst into a wildfire of terror, crying out in anguish, lamenting over your life and mourning your very self still seated - on the porch step. left out in the rain. on the edge of your very own heart. you were not meant for this. you were not meant to always be put last. it is okay to care for yourself. in fact, you should do this first. trust your gut. it's been there for you long before the lost souls have unraveled your magic only to leave it lying open on the ground, trampled on by those who don't know what they are looking for. reach out for yourself, sitting there, on the porch. give her a hug. take her hand and pull her back into your very own heart. find yourself, by yourself and lead yourself. you might find you need nothing more.

inside out

were you looking for a sparking match?
were you hoping for a flickering light?
were you dreaming of a billowing wildfire?
i hope not
you will not find that here
i am
the
pulsing
tenacious
slow-burning core of the earth
and you cannot extinguish my flames

she is the molten lava inside the volcano
she is the sweet nectar the bees desire
she is the clear water in your paper cup
she is the sultry tune played by street guitars
she is the pop of color in the local mural
she is the ripened fruit at the farmers' market
she is the beauty in the blooming flowers
she is the strength in the lioness' run
she is the guidance in the towering trees
she is the comfort in the ocean breeze
she is all that she could ever be
she is in everyone - in you - in me

inside out

i am of the sun
can't you see the flames?
i have been burning since birth
do not think you can calm the heat
do not think you can chill the roar
do you think i look ahead and cower in fear?
do you think i am afraid of what is next?
no
that is not me
i am of women before my time
i am of women who walked paths more trying
i am of women who will stop at nothing
i am of women who have conquered and reigned
i will not revolve around you
i do not need you to revolve around me
but -- you will see my orbit
you will respect my fire
or i will burn you down
(pele)

- elements, part four

meg junky

i can hear them
deep into the night
whispering
ancestors
they call upon me
spirits
they sing to me
dreams
they dance before me

i can't hide anymore

inside out

tears stream from my eyes
like stars falling from the sky
i am trying to let you go
burning your light out in the late night

meg junky

everything i have has been fought for

- woman

inside out

my dear
do you not remember
you came from a womb
you came from a garden for humans
you were delivered from the space
between a woman's legs
you were fed by her body
while you were tiny and helpless
you are forgetting where you came from
do you not remember
you came from a woman
you came from her

meg junky

may she forever keep
a curious mind
a beautiful heart
and a fiery soul

inside out

i am weightless in presence
a balloon
i float
up
up
up

i am worriless in release
a boulder
i sink
down
down
down

- mediation

meg junky

a mystery it is to me
why many clean
their houses and cars
their desks and closets
while many leave
their minds and bodies
their hearts and souls
unattended, cluttered and in disarray
over time it is impossible to find a thing
to sort through it all without frustrating
we are taught to clean the external
we should be taught to cleanse the internal
we need to practice yoga
we need to meditate
we long to sit in stillness
we long to release
we must learn this
we must find peace

inside out

someday
is today
not one of us knows
how many somedays
we get
so do it today

- what are you waiting for

meg junky

be like the sky
not like the weather
keep your mind
light as a feather

you can find peace
within this place
you simply have
to clear the space

inside out

you are a sum of your gifts
art lives within your soul
each moment you spend away from it
does not make you any less of an artist

- it is in your blood

meg junky

oh, the melancholy of a shared desire but he is nowhere to be found

inside out

i have been buried in the dark wet earth many
times and still i find the sun

meg junky

i travel in waves
i live in tumbling tides
i love in oceans
i fall from one to the next
i do not know how else to meet you
i have not lived any other way
and i have held my breath for so long
waiting

am i the only one left who can swim?

inside out

sometimes
in my dreams
you are so close
i can taste your smile
and breathe your laugh
it's funny how i know
this time would be different
i can feel it in my bones
the way you know you're home

meg junky

imagination is a close friend. she keeps me busy when i am anxious. she lies at the tip of my tongue like the dreams i almost give voice to but hesitate and withdraw. she paints my paintings first and sometimes that's where they stay. she comes up with words that become my poems, forever grateful i am for their honesty and courage. she creates plans both thoughtful and alluring and i execute them as i see fit. she dreams up all possibilities, no matter what it may take to achieve them. where to move. what project to start. who to call upon. and so on. she creates my living spaces, arranges books by color, furniture by style, records by genre and makes my home feel safe. she calls upon my soul to breathe into her my truth so she can examine my life and in what direction her vision should fly. she keeps me company when i am feeling out of place or in need of inspiration. she reminds me that it is never too late to make a change.
it is never too late to fly.

inside out

nothing wakes you up
quite like
writing the truth first thing in the morning
open the curtains
let it drip
from your heart
onto fresh pages
hold nothing back
trust me
the ink note
is stronger than a java jolt

meg junky

we play each other's instruments
like we've known how to all along
baby we make music

- duet

inside out

i open for you like an orchid
finally in bloom

meg junky

it's 6:15 am
i twist the blinds and crack the window
letting in the cool september air
i can feel the space where i am held
and reminded of what is ahead
i can sense the gentle suggestion that maybe it's
time to let the newness in
the harvest moon brings change
we know it will come just like every other year
and yet if we are not open to receive it
we might miss the magic floating in
on the autumn breeze among the golden rays
i don't want to miss the magic
i grab my sweater and step outside
breathing slowly
drinking in this delicate morning
i tell the wind i am ready
to twist
to open
i tell the morning
i am ready for the magic

inside out

with every word i write
a piece of armor shed
illusion undone
intimacy run
like needle through thread
what a new delight

meg junky

i see you standing there
in the dimly-lit doorway
a dream come true
my fingers tracing your outline
cologne-scented skin
warm
inviting
i breathe you in
you pull me closer
one touch
soft
enchanting
and i pray
i never wake up

inside out

when did i fall for your words
how they tap my heart
like raindrops on window sills
and strum it
like the strings of an acoustic guitar
i don't remember
how they came
or when
but they did
and i fell

meg junky

the trees come alive
when i walk under them with you
twisting
turning
bending
trying to look their best
even the forests know you are special

inside out

i find the way in which you fascinate me
to be quite enjoyable
utterly distracting
and good to the last drop

i have found heaven. i have seen it. i have felt it. i found it years ago when you said i love you and meant it. i found it one morning when the sunshine blessed the plants in my window. i found it as i practiced yoga surrounded by serenity and bliss. i found it at the concert last summer when the music brought tears to my eyes. i found it on the top of a mountain when i had never been higher. i found it bursting from the ripe fruit i ate by the water lakeside in the summertime. i found it when i was walking by the oak trees being blessed by the wind's breeze. i found it when we were underneath tangled sheets and nothing existed but us. i found it when there was nothing i could think of but your name. i found it walking down the street yesterday listening to a brand new album on repeat. i found it when you put your arm across me the other night as you fell asleep. i found it when you made me laugh so hard that breathing escaped me. i found it in poetry that gave me hope after a long year. i found it when i was dreaming last night and there was no worry in sight. i find heaven all the time. i see it. i feel it. i know where to look.

inside out

if i could tell you only one thing my dear, i would tell you this: you have everything you need.

meg junky

sister
you always had
good intentions
i see this
i am woman too
i will take your side
on the front lines
they do not see
what it takes
for us to walk
let alone stride
my dear
we are full of
great solutions

inside out

fear not
the sun will rise and set each day
nothing will lead you too far astray
far worse it would be to leave dreams behind
so follow your heart soul and mind

meg junky

you have had the same wallet
all these years
soft
brown
leather
and i smile
knowing my love note
on
bright
pink
paper
is carried with you
every single day

inside out

some days
the words spill out
like honey from a jar

the bees love them even more than you

meg junky

love is the way your eyes focus on mine the
moment you wake up

inside out

some mornings you stroke
my thighs
smooth like ponds of ice
winter

some afternoons you brush
my forearms
textured like freshly cut grass
spring

some evenings you caress
my shoulders
soft like the tulip petals
summer

some days you catch
all of me
weightless like falling leaves
autumn

meg junky

you bring the heat
the warming june
the scorching july
the melting august

and when i can barely breathe at all
you bring the rain
the cool sweet rain

i always liked thunderstorms

inside out

let me drink you in
slowly
swirl you across my tongue
gently
sip you and taste every bit of sweetness

- dessert wine | lovers

meg junky

your love
a hummingbird in flight
delicate
and unpredictable

inside out

i bathe in the goodness
like skin in coconut oil
the day fades and i see my sun
flickering through jade curtains
dancing on the windowsill
dusk lingers in the ocean air
tanned arms and sandy feet
i ne'er washed off the sea
salty curls and sun-kissed smirks
dancing along the beach
you stepping to the beat
our song on repeat
i feel at home

meg junky

writing to you
from a recipe of lines
delectable words
rich chocolate truffles
melting slowly in my mouth
as i read back to you
they swirl on my tongue
i soak in their sweetness
now that's dessert

inside out

your kisses
like the first day of summer
as sweet as the ripening berries
and as soft as the tulip petals
i want to eat them up
until i'm full

meg junky

you are the sun
and i am the moon
together we keep our world lit up

inside out

i hold you like my breath underwater

meg junky

your eyes tell me more than your lips ever could
in a language only we understand
i fall for you more than i should
far more than my heart may withstand

inside out

i remember the women. all of them. who have told me time and time again that in order to manifest your dreams you need to follow your truth and you will become them. at times it seems hard. we wonder where to start. it is as simple as this. you can start with your thoughts. your thoughts are energy. and because they are energy you will start to see the shift. your thoughts are your power. when you tell yourself and then the world what it is you are hungry for the signs start to appear. the right people show up. opportunities present to you seemingly unexpectedly but within this process you can see the source. the universe is magic. it will work in your favor. you can see what fits or does not. you can see who fits and who does not. the secret to this journey is intention. through this honesty you shall rise. i remember the women who have taught me. they have taught me the secret and now i can breathe deeply. i can find the magic. i can manifest.

meg junky

the most uplifting human beings i have ever met
have waded through the the darkest waters

- transmutation

inside out

ASPIRE
TO
INSPIRE
BEFORE
YOU
EXPIRE

meg junky

your potential
is like the horizon
you can see it
among the pink and orange sky
twirling among the clouds
but it stretches
far
far
far
greater
than you think

inside out

there is something to fall in love with in everyone
it just takes time

- patience

meg junky

i see color
it would be disrespectful to say i did not
but i see color
all colors
and see beauty
equal and brilliant

- respect

inside out

love
mirror on the wall
unfolding tales
exposing truths
not always what i want to see
but always what you hope to

- soulmate

meg junky

romance lives in the un-'s
the unspoken
the unseen
the unknown
it caresses you into the newness
with the hope that you might find
something you cannot do without
the unforgettable
the unbelievable
the unleavable

inside out

pupils expand
like clouds above
when we see
someone we love
if that is true
then my two
start to bloom
violet hues
when you walk
into a room

- calla lilies

meg junky

bathe in the fauna
drink in the sunlight
swim in the floral
dance in the daylight
dream near the fire
on this summer night
uncover your wishes
let them take flight

inside out

let me sit here
on the front porch
drink in the morning
until i am full of heaven

- summer

meg junky

your touch is like the scent of air
right before it rains

inside out

red roses flutter
her dress shimmers across the room
catching the golden hues
i recognize the sunshine
i have seen it in my dreams

sweet orchestral melodies
her dance echoes through the air
carrying an amber joy
i recognize the warmth
i have known it in my heart

rich hazel tones
her eyes meet mine in a moment
comforting my lonely heart
i recognize the love
i have waited all my life

meg junky

what could be more flattering
than to be named as one's muse
to ignite passion and creativity
in them like a fuse

inside out

maybe you came to inspire me again
to make me lift up the pen
to tell the world of your mystical existence and
the magical effect it has on me
to remind me that nothing
nothing
is ever really over
and we can always start again

meg junky

i am paralyzed in bliss
when his hands travel
to all the cities of my skin
kissing the roadmap of my body
from head to toe
this is where we are meant to live
please let this never end
let this bed be our home
i am mesmerized in this

inside out

nothing beats the combination of spanish guitar
a glass of red wine
and your hand
on the nape of my neck
caressing
undressing
my layers
as i let you closer and closer to my heart

meg junky

i know few gifts as precious as laughter

inside out

i am a glass of lemonade
in the july heat
you are the bee
buzzin' to a beat
you come here on sundays
where we always meet
you swirl the glass
till it settles nice and neat

meg junky

you make
my heart blush
my skin smile
my toes laugh
and
my soul dance

inside out

when i walk
it is with all the women
who have ever traveled the earth
circled the sun or graced the moon
for they are my history

when i rise
it is with the elemental energy
of our true mother
earth air water and fire
for they are within me

when i conquer
it is with my sisters
standing together as one
we do not fight alone
for together we are strong

when i love
it is with the ancient spirit
the goddess within
pure in its entirety
for this can heal us all

meg junky

each day i have taken for granted
i will repent for such ignorance
and kiss the toes of the sun
for his dedicated deliverance
i will grovel to the moon
and apologize to the trees
i will sing to the lakes
and dance with the bees
as quickly as the seasons change
i know all could end
the sun could set forever
and the roots could upend
i must call out to you
before it is too late
to thank you in sincerity
for all the magic you create

inside out

isn't it a beautiful thing
how you are out there living your life
and how i am here living mine
knowing what we had once upon a time
and that we couldn't last forever
even if we tried
it is all okay because we found another way
i hope you love your ocean view
and that you laugh every single day
i hope you smile in your sleep
as you dream beautiful dreams
you were one of a kind
i am sure you still are
i hope she knows like i did
and you have everything you ever wanted
because you deserve it
i hope you know like i do
so dream your beautiful dreams
as you breathe the ocean breeze
all year round

meg junky

if ever you unravel the guise of her eyes
you may find the nature of her mirth
and a boundless joy which underlies
the virtuous gravity of her worth

inside out

your body is your temple
adorned with delicate features and luscious curves
carrying happiness and joy
recycling fear and pain
it is your home
it is not theirs
remember this my dear
when they knock on the door
and try to enter your world
when they try to slide past
your feelings on the walls
when they try to hurdle over your stories of how
you came to be and why you can still breathe
remember this my dear
it is your home
it is not theirs
your body is your temple

meg junky

i never knew i could feel the fireworks
i never thought i could see the stars
i never dreamed i could travel to other galaxies

until i met you

and now
i travel boldly
and now
i see brightly
and now

i love

inside out

few things are shared between only two people
and oh what a treasure for it to be so

meg junky

rain trickles down the windows
the scent of hazelnut fills the room
coffee from the shop we love
we go there every week
sit at the same table
flowers in a vase
mason jar lattes
i steal glances from your hazel eyes
a sultry smile fills up your face
i think up pretty little words to say
about you and your hands
and how they hold mine
i can stay there all day
writing poems for you

inside out

to be vulnerable
is to be strong
it takes courage
to unlock your shutters
to open your blinds
to let another step
into the foyer of your heart
without slamming the door shut first in panic

meg junky

i only think about you when i'm breathing

inside out

the very thought of you leaves me entirely entranced and spectacularly spellbound. i want to breathe your air as your lips pull mine under. i can't seem to remember where we were going but instead let's just stay here. where time does not exist. our very own world. everything where it is supposed to be. you with me. clear as could be. we are some kind of fate. now i see.

meg junky

the lake was where we went when we were full
and wanted to be empty

and in emptying the weight
we instead became full

full of sunshine
and of light
and of joy

inside out

your *mood* lies in your *movement*

mind | body | soul

meg junky

like one magnet to another
i am pulled to the forest
captured
encompassed
drawn in by branches
fanned by leaves
sunlight peeks in
a dimly lit ballroom
where i can dance freely
the wind at my cheeks
while bluejays bustle
and monarchs meander
soft dirt paths give way
as i sway
no matter where i was headed
i stay
oh, the magic
here time slows
everything in its place
and so am i

inside out

have you ever been so sure
you were *meant* to know somebody

it is one of the most sure things of which i have
ever been convinced

meg junky

over and over
i imagine you in the doorway
except this time
i don't hesitate

inside out

you are the type
to write
spicy
poems about

i want to know what those words *taste* like

meg junky

my thoughts coherent
my sentences construed
worn like pendants
and carefully glued

upon the sight of you
entering the room
stutter, i do
a faltering flume

forgetting my speech
losing my lips
tongue out of reach
words become bricks

when you look at me
and smile
i am disarmed
and left beguiled

inside out

i realized then
the key was my pen
unlocking words of my heart

the ones i saved for you

meg junky

she you may not
pluck
for
she
is a wildflower

inside out

i am of the earth
filled with roaring seas and rich soil
with flowers and bees and turmoil

i am of the air
filled with endless breath and weightless sail
with vast depth and humbling vail

i am of the fire
filled with peaking flames and intensity
with little acclaim and scarcity

i am of the water
filled with tumultuous waves and endless shores
with countless saves and mighty scores

- elemental woman

meg junky

elements
one
two
three
and four
all rising inside my chest

inside out

your lips
an inch from mine
the strongest pull on earth

- magnetism

meg junky

i want to kiss you
everywhere
beneath the rose gold sunset
pull your hips toward mine
ocean waves
i want to forget my name
in your sea of sheets
soaking in the golden light
lovers tides

inside out

the sensuality of a moonlit sky
is a lovely accompaniment to your hand in mine

meg junky

today i am twenty-nine. here i stand - here i am remembering. looking back. looking ahead. the last of the twenties (my, how you've grown) my, how much has changed. i have waded. i have fought. i have climbed. i have come out the other side. softer. stronger. more resilient.
i can feel the magic in my hands and the wonder in my bones. it was not easy to get here. there were weeks of darkness. sometimes months. but now. now the sunshine pours.
an unending curiosity lies within that pitter-patters to the beat of my heart. i love in oceans. i dream in color. i write what i cannot always say. i mean what i do. i am ready for what is ahead. i am ready for what is next.

inside out

to find solace in impermanence
may be the greatest source of peace

meg junky

i am still learning
to hold and not grasp
to experience and not expect
to love and not fear
still i am

inside out

sunbeams stream from my eyes to yours
i recognize your light

meg junky

i want you to peel me apart layer by layer
i want you to know the beauty that lies within
i want you to feel the work that i have done
i want you to absorb the love from my skin
i want you to treat my body as a temple
i want you to sense the value in my smile
i want you to understand my pain unearthed
i want you to echo the joy in my healed heart
i want you to read my eyes and their language
i want you to witness my soul in all its light
i want you to see me inside out
and the magic that awaits when you do

inside out

life is about a lot less than you think it is
in the most harmonically beautiful way possible
and in the middle of this crystal lake
among the trees
sitting in a kayak
far away from everyone
you can feel from the water
the answers within
teaching and revealing
truths you have sought your whole life
for you are water too
healing and pure
herein lies the reminder to always trust yourself
and the subtleties of the universe
you must remember your power
i remember my power
all this time i was looking outward
and all i needed was within

meg junky

less expectation
more gratitude

- resolution

inside out

my language
has only one word for love
do you even know
how many kinds of love i have
for how many kinds of people
how are there no more words for love than one
it is the most important word that exists

- language barrier

meg junky

how rich might you be when your possessions are
stripped, your back bare and all has disappeared
but the sun?

will you hold yet
the known
the felt
the spirit

inside out

daydreaming of my
honeydew
marigold
sweet lavender love

meg junky

you taught me what it feels like
to love like it is an extension of your body
like my heart built another chamber
just for you
i think of you
as naturally as i think of myself
your needs are mine
i don't have to try
it comes effortlessly
let it always be this way
where i am yours
and you are mine

inside out

i have to believe that everything is happening the way it is meant to. my heart beats. my mind wonders. my soul pulls. the path before me winds, bends and twists, but i know these trials are lessons. all the great texts involve pain, hardship and overcoming great obstacles. i must not bow down to the challenges. i must not quiver. no. instead, i must rise. i must stand up and fight. with bravery and resilience. for my family. for my sisters and brothers and friends alike. we are tested every day. we are tested by people who have not yet found the light. we are tested by the patriarchy. we are tested by people who are threatened by others' differences instead of welcoming them. but you see, life is not meant to be lived in the darkness. life is not meant to keep you cowering from it, locked inside and being scared to breathe, scared to be yourself. no. life is meant to be lived. life is meant to be cannonballed into. to be sought with curiosity and determination. to be *lived*. so go. seek. do. travel. love. what are you waiting for?

meg junky

compassion
is the medicine
for all humanity
and it doesn't require
a health insurance plan

inside out

mantra for myself:
i will get out of my own way
i will make room for what is coming
i will breathe into the space

meg junky

the right kind of love will make you fall to your knees in gratitude thanking the earth, the sun, and the stars

the right kind of love will distract you from all else and make it impossible to leave

the right kind of love will make your heart feel like its traveled to other galaxies

the right kind of love will make you dance naked to every song you have ever fallen for

the right kind of love will make you sing all day every day, not just in the shower

the right kind of love will make your toes curl at the best times

the right kind of love will make you kiss and play and make love until your bones are tired and then do it all over again

inside out

the right kind of love will make you bless the
oxygen you breathe for allowing you to be here

the right kind of love will make you trust yourself
and never second guess your worth

the right kind of love will make your numbered
days feel infinite

the right kind of love will make your earthly
existence immortal

the right kind of love will make you apologize and
forgive naturally

the right kind of love will make you feel at home
and never alone

the right kind of love will make you see that you
have everything you need

the right kind of love is in you
the right kind of love is in me

meg junky

the sea level rises
the waves come
when you enter my ocean

- passion

inside out

how did you know ten years ago
that i would be this woman
you were the poetic fortune teller
and i the lead in your story
you said you could not wait to see
the woman i would become
i wonder what you would think of these thoughts
and these words all over these pages
my heart beats here
you were there when my poems were just seeds
and now they are a lush garden
i wish you could have seen the bloom

- growth

meg junky

few moments fill the space
quite like
crackling fire
flickering waves
and a cotton candy sky
after dinnertime
it is here i can slow down
and breathe

inside out

in the end all we have left
are the words we leave behind
on pages we hope they read
for they will keep us alive
long after we are gone

meg junky

thank you
for being sincerely interested
and for having a heart wide open.

treasure your softness.
cultivate your joy.
bask in your love.

do not let any of life's trials take these from you.
you, too, will be buried in the dark wet earth.
and you, too, will find the sun.

inside out

read + follow

web: megjunky.com
instagram: @megjunky
facebook: meg junky poetry

Made in the USA
Monee, IL
21 July 2020